Digital Marketing Growth Plan

Pam Billups

INTRODUCTION

This book is a supplement to the Web Growth Strategy Training and therefore, we will not go into every strategy in detail, rather, we will just summarize it in a manner that will be sufficient for you to be able to create a plan.

Before we get into your growth strategy, you really should spend some time on your product/service review and how your business fits into the market so that you can develop the best plan.

Your product or service must fit into the center of the 3 critical success factors, or you will struggle, no matter how much time and money you put into a plan. The 3 success factors are Knowledge, Passion, and Market.

If you don't have the Knowledge to do or sell what you provide, even if there is a strong market, you will struggle. If you don't have the Passion, you are destined to be miserable, no matter how much money you make.

The most important success factor by far is Market. You need a product or service that is needed and in demand in the market today. Please keep this in mind when you are looking at trends. Current trends are a good indication of marketability, but they can change frequently. You may need to adjust your product or service offering overtime just to keep up. In other words, what worked for you last year may not work this year.

So even if you have researched the market for your niche, please do a quick check and see if the demand is trending up or down and keep this in mind.

Make sure you are in your Sweet Spot

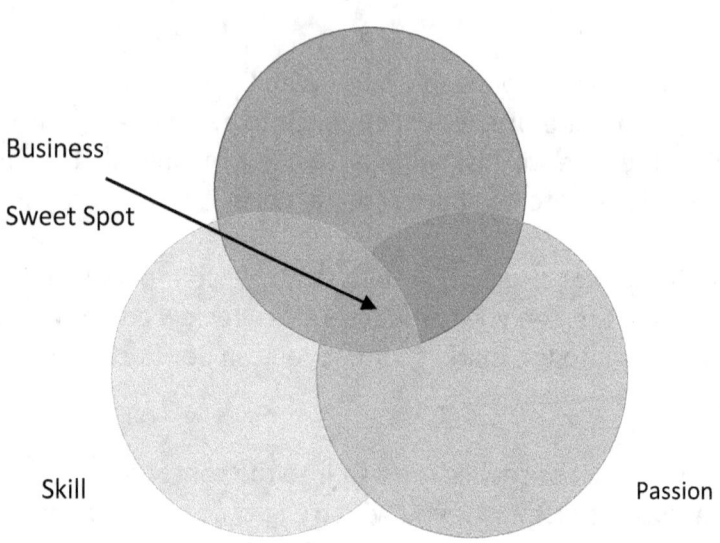

Market

Business

Sweet Spot

Skill

Passion

Do a quick check here.

Passion: Your WHY_____

Knowledge: What sets you apart_____

Market: What are the #s_____
# of Ads you see online, # of Competitors, # of similar product(s)
Don't be fooled, by your own idea. (no competition = no market)

USP = Unique Selling Proposition

This can be your Headline, Moto, Tag Line, or elevator speech.

What are the elements of your business that make you different from your competition?

_____

_____

Why are these relevant to your customer/prospect?

_____

_____

Where can you communicate each USP?

_____

_____

What are the top 3 benefits to buying online directly from your business?

_____

_____

_____

Complete your USP

I help (who)_____,

by (what)_____,

so that they can (benefit) _____.

There are so many choices available to a small business owner. With 100s of digital assets to choose from, you cannot maintain all of them until you can afford a team of people. Even then, it is a waste of time and money to support the assets that are not significantly contributing to your success. We are just going to focus on the core online strategies for a small business owner. You may want to expand the list based on your passion & knowledge, but this strategy will work for most of the entrepreneurs today.

Unless you have a large team, or a huge bank account, you should focus on no more than 2 or 3 of these any given week to truly expand your digital footprint. This workbook is set-up for 8 weeks of planning, which allows for all 8 strategies to be developed.

BENEFITS OF Web Marketing

More Leads & Higher ROI
Due to the minimal cost, social media is a viable way to connect with more potential customers and convert them into sales

Customer Satisfaction
Multiple platforms to answer customer questions and concerns

Higher Search Rankings
Social signals are a key factor in SEO and gaining more search engine visibility

Build Strong Partnerships
Many businesses seek to establish profitable partnerships with other businesses on social media

More Interaction & Engagement
Great way to stay in touch with your audience, as well as increased engagement and relationship building

Boosts Customer Loyalty
Consistent contact with your social audience will result in more customers doing repeat business

Multiple Platforms
Multiple social media sites for you to display your brand and connect with a new pool of customers and prospects

Online Reputation
Ability to build trust, credibility, and authority with your target market

5

Here is a suggested timeline for your Web Growth Strategy, to achieve Quick Results.

Even if you are on your 2nd, 3rd etc. weekly planning cycle, it is useful for continuous review and improvement. Don't skip this part, even if you believe you already have clear goals. Constant improvement is key.

Website Strategy

Social Strategy

Local / SEO Strategy

Email Strategy

Video Strategy

Referral Strategy

Reputation Strategy

What are your initial goals?

_____

_____

_____

Draw out an image or write some notes, on how your business will feel, after these goals are meet.

NOTES/IDEAS

Digital Marketing Plan

CHAPTER 1: WEBSITE STRATEGY

A good website strategy starts with reviewing these questions, even if you already have a website.

Background Information

1. Describe your target audience.

2. What is the purpose of the website?

3. What are your corporate core values and how do you express them to your visitors?

4. What makes you different from your competitors?

5. Why should people do business with you rather than your competitors?

6. Describe the style of the website you want.

7. Do you have specific company colors that need to be used?

8. What are your company colors?

9. Do you have any other materials that the site needs to match with in some way (brochures, press materials, etc.)?

If you don't yet have a website, skip questions 10-12.

10. *What do you like most about your current website?*

11. *Is there any functionality or options on your current website that you plan to keep (other than the content)?*

12. *What are your top 3 frustrations with your current website?*

13. What do your current competitors' websites have that you wish to have?

14. Are there any websites with designs that you like?

15. What about those websites would you like to be incorporated into your website?

16. What types of things do you see on other websites that you really like?

17. What types of things do you see on other websites that you really hate?

18. Name the 3 things that are most important in the design of your new website.

19. Name the 3 things that are least important in the design of your new website.

20. Who will be involved on your end in the website development?

21. Who or how will you be managing website upkeep?

22. Do you have a budget you are trying to meet?

Scope & Specs

23. Do you already have a URL (domain name) you plan to use? If not, do you need help selecting and registering a good URL?

    a. Find a short, easy name that matches your company feel. Include Keywords if possible.

24. Do you have a logo you plan to use, or will one need to be created?

25. If you have one, do you own original artwork files?

26. Will you need a favicon created (that image on a desktop tab)?

27. Do you have a tagline you wish to use, or do you need help creating one for your site?

28. Do you have a completed site layout for the new website?

29. How many pages will the finished website be (estimated)?

30. Do you have any page layouts complete?

31. Do you have the content or will content need content creation services?

32. How many pages of content will need to be developed?

33. Will there be any cross promotion of content within the site?

34. Will you require help with importing and formatting your content?

35. Do you need training for making website updates, content etc.?

Actions

36. What types of actions do you want your visitors to take on your website?

37. Do you have any specific photos you plan to use?

38. Do you have full rights to those files?

39. Do you have hi-res files of your images?

40. Will you need to find and/or create any images for the website?

41. Will video or audio be a part of the new website?

42. How many videos or audio files will be added and/or created?

43. Do you require online chat features?

44. Do you have any other media or PDF documents that need to be incorporated, or will any need to be created?

45. Will these need to be optimized for search?

46. Will your visitors require any special needs (screen reader, larger fonts)?

47. Do you have any specific mobile requirements?

48. Do you need multi-language support?

Systems

49. Will you need a shopping cart system for e-commerce?

50. Do you have a system you already use?

51. Do you need a content management system?

52. Do you prefer a particular CMS to use? (i.e., WordPress)

53. Will you need multiple levels of access?

54. Do you need to be able to manage content publishing approval?

55. Does your site need a blog or a forum?

56. Will users need to log in to your site for any reason?

57. If so, why?

58. Do you need any password protected areas?

59. What kind of content will be put behind password protected areas?

60. How many web forms does your new site need?

61. What is the purpose of each?

62. How do you want the submitted info handled? (email, database)

63. Do you need any social sharing features built in?

64. Will there be any third-party applications that will need to be integrated? (i.e. Mailchimp, hotjar)

65. What are they?

66. Will you need an events calendar feature?

67. Do you have any subscription services?

68. Do you use a third party for any part of subscription content delivery and/or payment?

69. Do you require printer friendly options?

70. Do you wish to employ any "content-on-demand" features (i.e., hidden elements that are made visible with certain actions)?

71. Do you want a fixed-width or fluid-width design?

72. What information must be on the home page?

73. What information must always be visible?

74. What features, sections or information do you want emphasized on the site?

75. Will different sections have different designs, layouts or coloring?

76. Do you have any flash elements you want included?

77. Are those done, or do they need to be created?

78. Do you need an internal site search feature?

79. Do you want contact phone numbers prominently displayed?

80. Will you be offering advertising on the site?

81. How should that be implemented?

82. Do you have a Google Analytics account?

83. What is your time frame for total project completion?

84. What keywords will your customers be searching for?

8 Elements of a Website

WEBSITE VISITOR ACTION PROCESS

Opt-In
Opt-in For Free Information & Discounts

Social Media
Social Media Interaction (Share Content & Follow)

Products & Services
Review Product & Service Offerings

Contact or Visit You
Contact Or Visit You To Get More Info

Content
Read Helpful & Engaging Content

Make A Purchase
Purchase Desired Product or Service

Navigation
Navigate to Get a Feel For Your Company

Refer Others
Tell Other People About Your Business

Set <u>Smart</u> Goals for your Website

What Are S.M.A.R.T. Goals?

S.M.A.R.T. goals are a simple way to improve the odds of success with regards to achieving a goal.

The acronym stands for:

S – Specific

When defining your goal, be very specific about what you need to achieve. Consider this the statement of purpose for your goal. It should incorporate a response to the famous 'w' questions:

- Who – Consider who should be included to accomplish the goal.
- What – Think about exactly what you need to achieve, and don't be general.
- When – This is detailed in the Time-based portion of your goal.
- Where – Where is this located?
- Why – What is the purpose behind your goal?

M – Measurable

What measurements would you say you will use to decide whether you've met you goal? This makes an objective a more finite one the because it gives an approach to quantify success. How much? How many? How will you know when it is accomplished?

A – Achievable

Consider if you have the finances or skills required. On the off chance that you don't, consider what you would need to accomplish the tasks needed to complete your goal.

R – Realistic (Relevant)

This pertains to whether the goal is reasonable and results-based. It needs to have results that tie directly back to the more extensive business objectives.

T – Time-Based

Anybody can set objectives, however if doesn't have a realistic timeline, odds are you're not going to succeed. Setting a deadline to individual task is key. If a task is going to take a long time, break it up into smaller tasks, and set time-based goals, so that you have reasonable milestones to focus on. Giving time requirements also creates a sense of urgency.

Make Some Goals for your Website

Area	Current	Future
Navigation		
Content		
Products & Services		
Opt-in		
Social Media		
Contact or Visit You		
Make a Purchase		
Refer Others		

Big Website GOAL _____

STEPS TO TAKE (ACTION)	BY WHEN	⊕

SMART GOALS – Specific, Measurable, Realistic, Achievable, Time-based.

What can you learn, outsource, simplify, automate or eliminate?

KEYS TO SUCCEESS (TASK)	WHO CAN HELP?	⊕

Daily Plan

Date

7a	
30	
8	
30	
9	
30	
10	
30	
11	
30	
12	
30	
1	
30	
2	
30	
3	
30	
4	
30	
5	
30	
6	

Healthy Habits

Exercise: _____ Mins

Water ○ ○ ○ ○ ○ ○ ○ ○

Must Do

To Do

Routine Tasks

Errands / Appointments

Daily Plan

Date

M T W Th F Sa Su

Must Do

_____

_____

_____

_____

_____

To Do

_____

_____

_____

_____

Routine Tasks

_____

_____

_____

_____

Errands / Appointments

_____

_____

_____

_____

7a _____

30 _____

8 _____

30 _____

9 _____

30 _____

10 _____

30 _____

11 _____

30 _____

12 _____

30 _____

1 _____

30 _____

2 _____

30 _____

3 _____

30 _____

4 _____

30 _____

5 _____

30 _____

6 _____

Healthy Habits

Exercise: _____ Mins

Water O O O O O O O O

Daily Plan

Date   M   T W Th F Sa Su

7a ....

  30 ....

8 ....

  30 ....

9 ....

  30 ....

10 ....

  30 ....

11 ....

  30 ....

12 ....

  30 ....

1 ....

  30 ....

2 ....

  30 ....

3 ....

  30 ....

4 ....

  30 ....

5 ....

  30 ....

6 ....

Healthy Habits

Exercise: _____ Mins

Water O O O O O O O O

Must Do

To Do

Routine Tasks

Errands / Appointments

Daily Plan

Date   M T W Th F Sa Su

Must Do

7a ....

  30 _____

8 _____

  30 _____

9 _____

  30 _____

10 _____

  30 _____

11 _____

  30 _____

12 _____

  30 _____

1 _____

  30 _____

2 _____

  30 _____

3 _____

  30 _____

4 _____

  30 _____

5 _____

  30 _____

6 _____

To Do

Routine Tasks

Errands / Appointments

Healthy Habits

Exercise: _____ Mins

Water O O O O O O O O

Daily Plan

Date   M T W Th F Sa Su

7a ....

  30 ....

8 ....

  30 ....

9 ....

  30 ....

10 ....

  30 ....

11 ....

  30 ....

12 ....

  30 ....

1 ....

  30 ....

2 ....

  30 ....

3 ....

  30 ....

4 ....

  30 ....

5 ....

  30 ....

6 ....

Healthy Habits

Exercise: _____ Mins

Water ⭕⭕⭕⭕⭕⭕⭕⭕

Must Do

To Do

Routine Tasks

Errands / Appointments

Daily Plan

Date   M   T   W   Th   F   Sa   Su

Must Do

7a _____

  30 _____

8 _____

  30 _____

9 _____

  30 _____

To Do

10 _____

  30 _____

11 _____

  30 _____

12 _____

  30 _____

1 _____

Routine Tasks

  30 _____

2 _____

  30 _____

3 _____

  30 _____

4 _____

  30 _____

5 _____

Errands / Appointments

  30 _____

6 _____

Healthy Habits

Exercise: _____ Mins

Water O O O O O O O O

Daily Plan

Date

M T W Th F Sa Su

7a	
30	
8	
30	
9	
30	
10	
30	
11	
30	
12	
30	
1	
30	
2	
30	
3	
30	
4	
30	
5	
30	
6	

Must Do

To Do

Routine Tasks

Errands / Appointments

Healthy Habits

Exercise: _____ Mins

Water O O O O O O O O

_____ Week in Review

Top 3: Key Performance Indicators
These are the key measurables that are going to move the needle.

#1 Goal_____

Last Week | What must you do differently?

#2 Goal_____

Last Week | What must you do differently?

#3 Goal_____

Last Week | What must you do differently?

CHAPTER 2: CONTENT STRATEGY

Content is defined as the principal substance (such as written matter, illustrations, or music) offered by a website. Your content is a reflection of you and your busines, so it needs to be consistent with the theme, colors and style of the business.

This is also a good time to ensure your content works will on mobile, which is a different version of your desktop website that is designed to be viewed specifically on mobile devices.

They usually contain a limited number of pages, images, and content in order to quickly provide mobile users with the information they need.

WHY A MOBILE WEBSITE IS A PRIORITY

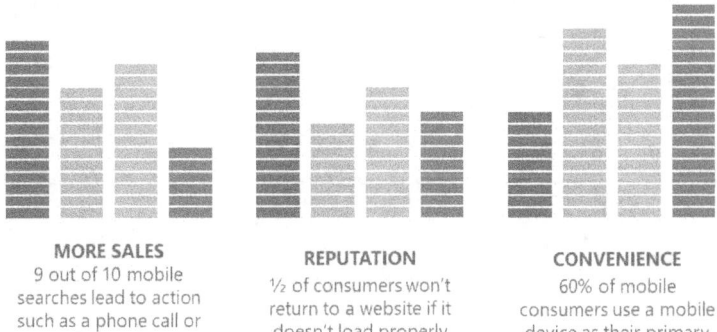

MORE SALES
9 out of 10 mobile searches lead to action such as a phone call or store visit

REPUTATION
½ of consumers won't return to a website if it doesn't load properly on their mobile devices

CONVENIENCE
60% of mobile consumers use a mobile device as their primary or exclusive internet source

Make Some Content Goals

Media	Current	Future
About/Bio Page		
Products & Services		
Terms & Privacy		
Pricing Page		
Product Images		
Lead Magnet		
Others		

Big Social GOAL _____

STEPS TO TAKE (ACTION)	BY WHEN	⊕

SMART GOALS – Specific, Measurable, Realistic, Achievable, Time-based.

What can you learn, outsource, simplify, automate or eliminate?

KEYS TO SUCCEESS (TASK)	WHO CAN HELP?	⊕

Daily Plan

Date

Must Do

_____
_____
_____
_____
_____

To Do

_____
_____
_____
_____

7a _____

30 _____

8 _____

30 _____

9 _____

30 _____

10 _____

30 _____

11 _____

30 _____

12 _____

30 _____

1 _____

30 _____

2 _____

30 _____

3 _____

30 _____

4 _____

30 _____

5 _____

30 _____

6 _____

Routine Tasks

_____
_____
_____
_____

Errands / Appointments

_____
_____
_____
_____

Healthy Habits

Exercise: _____ Mins

Water ⭕⭕⭕⭕⭕⭕⭕⭕

Daily Plan

Date

M T W Th F Sa Su

Must Do

7a _____

30 _____

8 _____

30 _____

9 _____

30 _____

To Do

10 _____

30 _____

11 _____

30 _____

12 _____

30 _____

1 _____

30 _____

Routine Tasks

2 _____

30 _____

3 _____

30 _____

4 _____

30 _____

5 _____

30 _____

Errands / Appointments

6 _____

Healthy Habits

Exercise: _____ Mins

Water ○ ○ ○ ○ ○ ○ ○ ○

Daily Plan

Date   M T W Th F Sa Su

Must Do

7a	
30	
8	
30	
9	

To Do

30	
10	
30	
11	
30	
12	
30	

Routine Tasks

1	
30	
2	
30	
3	
30	

Errands / Appointments

4	
30	
5	
30	
6	

Healthy Habits

Exercise: _____ Mins

Water ⭘ ⭘ ⭘ ⭘ ⭘ ⭘ ⭘

Daily Plan

Date   M   T W Th F Sa Su

Must Do

7a	_____
30	_____
8	_____
30	_____
9	_____
30	_____
10	_____
30	_____
11	_____
30	_____
12	_____
30	_____
1	_____
30	_____
2	_____
30	_____
3	_____
30	_____
4	_____
30	_____
5	_____
30	_____
6	_____

To Do

Routine Tasks

Errands / Appointments

Healthy Habits

Exercise: _____ Mins

Water ⭘ ⭘ ⭘ ⭘ ⭘ ⭘ ⭘ ⭘

Daily Plan

Date   M T W Th F Sa Su

Must Do

7a _____

  30 _____

8 _____

  30 _____

9 _____

  30 _____

To Do

10 _____

  30 _____

11 _____

  30 _____

12 _____

  30 _____

Routine Tasks

1 _____

  30 _____

2 _____

  30 _____

3 _____

  30 _____

4 _____

  30 _____

5 _____

Errands / Appointments

  30 _____

6 _____

Healthy Habits

Exercise: _____ Mins

Water O O O O O O O O

Daily Plan

Date   M T W Th F Sa Su

7a

30

8

30

9

30

10

30

11

30

12

30

1

30

2

30

3

30

4

30

5

30

6

Healthy Habits

Exercise: _____ Mins

Water O O O O O O O O

Must Do

To Do

Routine Tasks

Errands / Appointments

Daily Plan

Date

7a _____

  30 _____

8 _____

  30 _____

9 _____

  30 _____

10 _____

  30 _____

11 _____

  30 _____

12 _____

  30 _____

1 _____

  30 _____

2 _____

  30 _____

3 _____

  30 _____

4 _____

  30 _____

5 _____

  30 _____

6 _____

Healthy Habits

Exercise: _____ Mins

Water O O O O O O O O

Must Do

_____
_____
_____
_____
_____

To Do

_____
_____
_____
_____

Routine Tasks

_____
_____
_____
_____

Errands / Appointments

_____
_____
_____
_____

_____ Week in Review

Top 3: Key Performance Indicators
These are the key measurables that are going to move the needle.

#1 Goal_____

Last Week   What must you do differently?

[ ] $\Longrightarrow$ [ ]

#2 Goal_____

Last Week   What must you do differently?

[ ] $\Longrightarrow$ [ ]

#3 Goal_____

Last Week   What must you do differently?

[ ] $\Longrightarrow$ [ ]

Digital Marketing Plan

CHAPTER 3: SOCIAL MEDIA

Social media is simply "media for social interaction and communication," which usually occurs on sites such as Facebook, Twitter, LinkedIn, Pinterest, Instagram and more.

Social Media Marketing is the practice of building a company's social media presence with the goal of ultimately converting those connections into sales.

There are 100s of social media sites online today, and it is a waste of time to be on all of them. Unless you have a large team or deep packets, pick 1 or 2 and develop a strategy around those to start. If you create a social profile and do nothing with it, it can be worse for your reputation than not being on the platform at all.

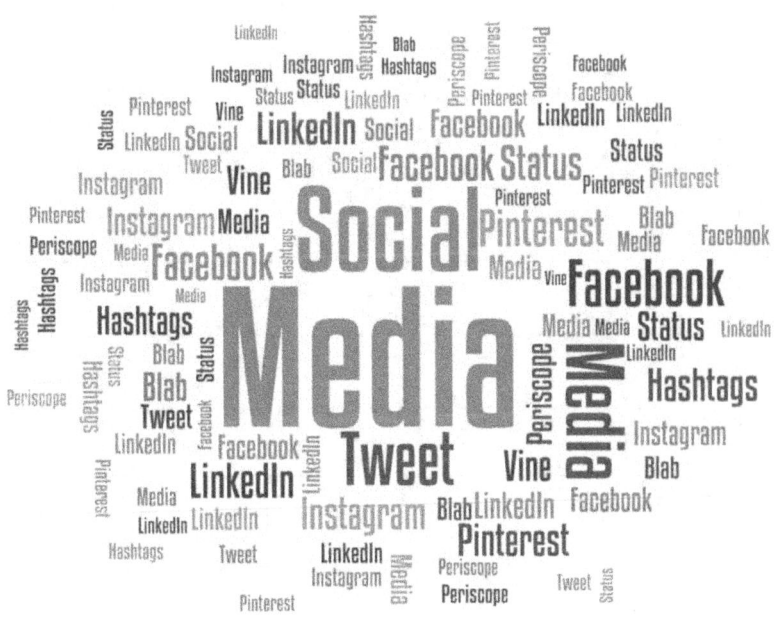

You need to research your customer base and see where they are, because that matters more than which one is the biggest. Be where your customers are.

Make Some Social Goals

Media	Current	Future
Facebook Page		
Facebook Group		
YouTube Channel		
LinkedIn		
Pinterest		
Instagram		
Others		

Big Social GOAL _____

STEPS TO TAKE (ACTION)	BY WHEN	⊕

SMART GOALS – Specific, Measurable, Realistic, Achievable, Time-based.

What can you learn, outsource, simplify, automate or eliminate?

KEYS TO SUCCEESS (TASK)	WHO CAN HELP?	⊕

Daily Plan

Date _____ M T W Th F Sa Su

7a _____	

Must Do

_____

_____

_____

_____

To Do

_____

_____

_____

_____

Routine Tasks

_____

_____

_____

_____

Errands / Appointments

_____

_____

_____

_____

7a _____
30 _____
8 _____
30 _____
9 _____
30 _____
10 _____
30 _____
11 _____
30 _____
12 _____
30 _____
1 _____
30 _____
2 _____
30 _____
3 _____
30 _____
4 _____
30 _____
5 _____
30 _____
6 _____

Healthy Habits

Exercise: _____ Mins
Water ⚫ ⚪ ⚪ ⚪ ⚪ ⚪ ⚪ ⚪

44

Daily Plan

Date

M T W Th F Sa Su

7a
30
8
30
9
30
10
30
11
30
12
30
1
30
2
30
3
30
4
30
5
30
6

Must Do

To Do

Routine Tasks

Errands / Appointments

Healthy Habits

Exercise: _____ Mins

Water O O O O O O O O

Daily Plan

Date　　　　M T W Th F Sa Su

Must Do

7a _____

　30 _____

8 _____

　30 _____

9 _____

　30 _____

To Do

10 _____

　30 _____

11 _____

　30 _____

12 _____

　30 _____

1 _____

　30 _____

Routine Tasks

2 _____

　30 _____

3 _____

　30 _____

4 _____

　30 _____

5 _____

Errands / Appointments

　30 _____

6 _____

Healthy Habits

Exercise: _____ Mins

Water ○ ○ ○ ○ ○ ○ ○ ○

Daily Plan

Date   M   T W Th F Sa Su

7a	## Must Do
30	
8	
30	
9	
30	## To Do
10	
30	
11	
30	
12	
30	
1	## Routine Tasks
30	
2	
30	
3	
30	
4	
30	## Errands / Appointments
5	
30	
6	

Healthy Habits

Exercise: _____ Mins
Water O O O O O O O O

Daily Plan

Date   M T W Th F Sa Su

7a	
30	
8	
30	
9	
30	
10	
30	
11	
30	
12	
30	
1	
30	
2	
30	
3	
30	
4	
30	
5	
30	
6	

Must Do

To Do

Routine Tasks

Errands / Appointments

Healthy Habits

Exercise: _____ Mins

Water O O O O O O O O

Daily Plan

Date   M T W Th F Sa Su

7a _____	**Must Do**
30 _____	_____
8 _____	_____
30 _____	_____
9 _____	_____
30 _____	_____
10 _____	**To Do**
30 _____	_____
11 _____	_____
30 _____	_____
12 _____	_____
30 _____	**Routine Tasks**
1 _____	_____
30 _____	_____
2 _____	_____
30 _____	_____
3 _____	**Errands / Appointments**
30 _____	_____
4 _____	_____
30 _____	_____
5 _____	_____
30 _____	
6 _____	

Healthy Habits

Exercise: _____ Mins

Water ⭘ ⭘ ⭘ ⭘ ⭘ ⭘ ⭘ ⭘

Daily Plan

Date   M   T   W   Th   F   Sa   Su

7a _____

  30 _____

8 _____

  30 _____

9 _____

  30 _____

10 _____

  30 _____

11 _____

  30 _____

12 _____

  30 _____

1 _____

  30 _____

2 _____

  30 _____

3 _____

  30 _____

4 _____

  30 _____

5 _____

  30 _____

6 _____

Healthy Habits

Exercise: _____ Mins

Water O O O O O O O O

Must Do

_____

_____

_____

_____

To Do

_____

_____

_____

_____

Routine Tasks

_____

_____

_____

_____

Errands / Appointments

_____

_____

_____

_____

_____ Week in Review

Top 3: Key Performance Indicators
These are the key measurables that are going to move the needle.

#1 Goal_____

Last Week   What must you do differently?

#2 Goal_____

Last Week   What must you do differently?

#3 Goal_____

Last Week   What must you do differently?

CHAPTER 4: LOCAL STRATEGY

Local SEO is the process of optimizing a website to come up in the search engine results when users enter "localized" keywords and phrases into the internet search engines – such as Google, Yahoo, and Bing.

For example:
"Cosmetic Dentist in Rochester, NY"

97% of consumers use the internet to search for local products and services. If you are a local provider, you need a good strategy around your local market. This is typically done through quality site content and blogging.

List out the cities, areas and keywords where you know your customers are looking for your service. Then find out where you rank, either by doing a search online, by analyzing your traffic through google analytics, or a keyword ranking tool.

Remember that there are companies that spend big money to rank higher than you. Just because you are on the first page today does not mean someone will not push you off the next week. This requires consistent work, but the payoff is saving $1000s per year in paid ad spend.

This is an area of marketing where there are a lot of bad practices that can get your site flagged or de-ranked, so make sure you do your research. Good content on your site which is helpful to the local market is always good practice.

Make Some Local Goals

Search Term	Current	Future
Product + City		
Service + County/State		
Google Maps		
Yahoo		
Bing		
Local Listings		
Local Events		

Big Local Marketing GOAL _____

STEPS TO TAKE (ACTION)	BY WHEN	⊕

SMART GOALS – Specific, Measurable, Realistic, Achievable, Time-based.

What can you learn, outsource, simplify, automate or eliminate?

KEYS TO SUCCEESS (TASK)	WHO CAN HELP?	⊕

Daily Plan

Date   M T W Th F Sa Su

Must Do

7a

30

8

30

9

30

10

30

11

30

12

30

1

30

2

30

3

30

4

30

5

30

6

To Do

Routine Tasks

Errands / Appointments

Healthy Habits

Exercise: _____ Mins

Water ⭕ ⭕ ⭕ ⭕ ⭕ ⭕ ⭕ ⭕

Daily Plan

Date   M T W Th F Sa Su

7a	
30	
8	
30	
9	
30	
10	
30	
11	
30	
12	
30	
1	
30	
2	
30	
3	
30	
4	
30	
5	
30	
6	

Healthy Habits

Exercise: _____ Mins

Water O O O O O O O O

Must Do

To Do

Routine Tasks

Errands / Appointments

Daily Plan

Date   M   T W Th F Sa Su

Must Do

7a

  30

8

  30

9

  30

To Do

10

  30

11

  30

12

  30

1

  30

Routine Tasks

2

  30

3

  30

4

  30

5

  30

Errands / Appointments

6

Healthy Habits

Exercise: _____ Mins

Water O O O O O O O O

Daily Plan

Date

	Must Do
7a	
30	
8	
30	
9	
30	To Do
10	
30	
11	
30	
12	
30	
1	
30	Routine Tasks
2	
30	
3	
30	
4	
30	
5	Errands / Appointments
30	
6	

Healthy Habits

Exercise: _____ Mins
Water ⭕⭕⭕⭕⭕⭕⭕⭕

Daily Plan

Date
M T W Th F Sa Su

Must Do

7a

30

8

30

9

30

10

30

11

30

12

30

1

30

To Do

2

30

3

30

Routine Tasks

4

30

5

30

6

Errands / Appointments

Healthy Habits

Exercise: _____ Mins

Water O O O O O O O O

Daily Plan

Date   M T W Th F Sa Su

Must Do

7a	
30	
8	
30	
9	
30	
10	
30	
11	
30	
12	
30	
1	
30	
2	
30	
3	
30	
4	
30	
5	
30	
6	

To Do

Routine Tasks

Errands / Appointments

Healthy Habits

Exercise: _____ Mins

Water ⭘ ⭘ ⭘ ⭘ ⭘ ⭘ ⭘ ⭘

Daily Plan

Date _____ M T W Th F Sa Su

Must Do

7a _____
  30 _____
8 _____
  30 _____
9 _____
  30 _____

To Do

10 _____
  30 _____
11 _____
  30 _____
12 _____
  30 _____
1 _____
  30 _____

Routine Tasks

2 _____
  30 _____
3 _____
  30 _____
4 _____
  30 _____
5 _____

Errands / Appointments

  30 _____
6 _____

Healthy Habits

Exercise: _____ Mins
Water ○ ○ ○ ○ ○ ○ ○ ○

_____ Week in Review

Top 3: Key Performance Indicators
These are the key measurables that are going to move the needle.

#1 Goal_____

Last Week | What must you do differently?

#2 Goal_____

Last Week | What must you do differently?

#3 Goal_____

Last Week | What must you do differently?

PREP WORK FOR NEXT 4 WEEKS

Now that you are well into your website, local and social strategies, it is time to look back and forward at your goals. You might have exceeded your expectations, but if you're like most, you are struggling with at least one, if not all the goals.

This is very common, and part of your strategy is to always conduct a check and review, regroup and adjust. This is how to get past the roadblocks all small business must overcome.

Update and Improve your Goals

Area	Current	Future
Website		
Local		
Social		
Video		
Email		

Notes:

4 MAJOR ROADBLOCKS

Ineffective Marketing

Do traditional marketing methods continue to drain your budget even though they're ineffective?

Stiff Competition

Do you feel like your closest competitors are taking your fair share of the market?

Digital Technology

Are you struggling to grasp and implement proven new-age marketing strategies?

Lack of Time

Are you putting off Online Marketing because you feel that you just don't have the time?

Big 3 GOALs #1_____

Big 3 GOALs #2_____

Big 3 GOALs #3_____

Big Milestones (ACTION)	B Y W H E N	⊕

SMART GOALS – Specific, Measurable, Realistic, Achievable, Time-based.

What can you learn, outsource, simplify, automate or eliminate?

KEYS TO SUCCEESS (TASK)	WHO CAN HELP?	⊕

Make Notes in your plan to Achieve your Goals

Su	M	T	W	Th	F	Sa

Big Weekly Plans

Week	Most Important Task of each Week
1	
2	
3	
4	

Notes:

Make Notes in your plan to Achieve your Goals

KPIs	Goal	WK1	WK2	WK3	WK4
Traffic					
Leads					
Sales					
Gross Revenue					
Social KPI					
Local KPI					
Page #1					
# of Online Assets					

Notes:

Digital Marketing Plan

CHAPTER 5: EMAIL STRATEGY

Email Marketing is the practice of sending both sales and non-sales messages to a list of email subscribers. Sent via the internet, this method allows you to quickly get your marketing messages in front of a highly-targeted audience – consistently.

This is an area of marketing where there are a lot of bad practices that can get your site flagged or de-ranked, so make sure you do your research. Good content on your site that is helpful to the local market is always good.

Make Some Email Marketing Goals

Area	Current	Future
CRM system		
Opt-in		
Newsletter		
Sign-up incentive		
Welcome email		
Follow-up		
Open Rate		

WHY EMAIL MARKETING IS A **PRIORITY**

44% Of Email
Marketing Recipients
Make Purchases Based
On The Email Promo

91% Of People Check
Their Emails At Least
Once Per Day

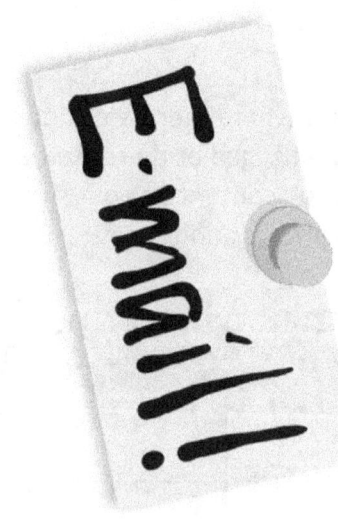

Email Marketing Returns
An Average Of Over $44
for Every $1 Spent

72% Of Consumers Sign
Up To Email Lists To Get
Discounts

60% Of Marketers Say
Email Marketing Is
Producing A ROI

72

Big Email GOAL _____

STEPS TO TAKE (ACTION)	BY WHEN	⊕

SMART GOALS – Specific, Measurable, Realistic, Achievable, Time-based.

What can you learn, outsource, simplify, automate or eliminate?

KEYS TO SUCCEESS (TASK)	WHO CAN HELP?	⊕

Daily Plan

Date   M   T W Th F Sa Su

7a _____

  30 _____

8 _____

  30 _____

9 _____

  30 _____

10 _____

  30 _____

11 _____

  30 _____

12 _____

  30 _____

1 _____

  30 _____

2 _____

  30 _____

3 _____

  30 _____

4 _____

  30 _____

5 _____

  30 _____

6 _____

Healthy Habits

Exercise: _____ Mins

Water ○ ○ ○ ○ ○ ○ ○ ○

Must Do

_____
_____
_____
_____

To Do

_____
_____
_____
_____

Routine Tasks

_____
_____
_____
_____

Errands / Appointments

_____
_____
_____
_____

Daily Plan

Date M T W Th F Sa Su

	## Must Do

7a ....

30 ....

8 ....

30 ....

9 ....

30 ....

10 ....

30 ....

11 ....

30 ....

12 ....

30 ....

1 ....

30 ....

2 ....

30 ....

3 ....

30 ....

4 ....

30 ....

5 ....

30 ....

6 ....

Healthy Habits

Exercise: _____ Mins

Water O O O O O O O O

To Do

Routine Tasks

Errands / Appointments

Daily Plan

Date M T W Th F Sa Su

Must Do

7a ....

  30 ....

8 ....

  30 ....

9 ....

  30 ....

10 ....

  30 ....

11 ....

  30 ....

12 ....

  30 ....

To Do

1 ....

  30 ....

2 ....

  30 ....

3 ....

  30 ....

Routine Tasks

4 ....

  30 ....

5 ....

  30 ....

6 ....

Errands / Appointments

Healthy Habits

Exercise: _____ Mins

Water O O O O O O O O

Daily Plan

Date

Must Do

7a ....

30 ....

8 ....

30 ....

9 ....

30 ....

To Do

10 ....

30 ....

11 ....

30 ....

12 ....

30 ....

1 ....

Routine Tasks

30 ....

2 ....

30 ....

3 ....

30 ....

4 ....

30 ....

5 ....

Errands / Appointments

30 ....

6 ....

Healthy Habits

Exercise: _____ Mins

Water ○ ○ ○ ○ ○ ○ ○ ○

Daily Plan

Date _____

Time	
7a	
30	
8	
30	
9	
30	
10	
30	
11	
30	
12	
30	
1	
30	
2	
30	
3	
30	
4	
30	
5	
30	
6	

Healthy Habits

Exercise: _____ Mins

Water ⭘ ⭘ ⭘ ⭘ ⭘ ⭘ ⭘

Must Do

To Do

Routine Tasks

Errands / Appointments

Daily Plan

Date   M T W Th F Sa Su

Must Do

7a

30

8

30

9

30

10

30

11

30

12

30

1

30

2

30

3

30

4

30

5

30

6

To Do

Routine Tasks

Errands / Appointments

Healthy Habits

Exercise: _____ Mins

Water O O O O O O O O

Daily Plan

Date   M   T W Th F Sa Su

Must Do

7a _____

30 _____

8 _____

30 _____

9 _____

30 _____

To Do

10 _____

30 _____

11 _____

30 _____

12 _____

30 _____

1 _____

Routine Tasks

30 _____

2 _____

30 _____

3 _____

30 _____

4 _____

Errands / Appointments

30 _____

5 _____

30 _____

6 _____

Healthy Habits

Exercise: _____ Mins

Water ⭕ ⭕ ⭕ ⭕ ⭕ ⭕ ⭕ ⭕

_____ Week in Review

Top 3: Key Performance Indicators
These are the key measurables that are going to move the needle.

#1 Goal_____

Last Week   What must you do differently?

#2 Goal_____

Last Week   What must you do differently?

#3 Goal_____

Last Week   What must you do differently?

Digital Marketing Plan

CHAPTER 6: VIDEO STRATEY

Video Marketing is necessary in today's market, but don't worry that doesn't mean you have to be on camera. There are many methods to produce video content for your product or service, and most of them do not require face time.

If you would like to be in front of the camera, all the better. Personal time virtually interacting with your future customers really helps with likability and helps people feel like they know you.

YouTube and Facebook are both big in video preferencing, but there are 100s of other video platforms that you can repurpose your content in, too.

Make Some Video Goals

Area	Current	Future
Facebook		
YouTube		
Instagram		
Frequency		
# of Videos		
Optimizing		

WHY VIDEO MARKETING IS A PRIORITY

100 million internet users watch videos online every day

It is 50x easier to achieve a page 1 ranking on Google with a video

Blog posts incorporating video attract three times as many inbound links as blog posts without video

YouTube users spend more than 6 billion hours watching videos each month

The average user spends 88% more time on a website with video

Big Video GOAL _____

STEPS TO TAKE (ACTION)	BY WHEN	⊕

SMART GOALS – Specific, Measurable, Realistic, Achievable, Time-based.

What can you learn, outsource, simplify, automate or eliminate?

KEYS TO SUCCEESS (TASK)	WHO CAN HELP?	⊕

Daily Plan

Date   M T W Th F Sa Su

7a	## Must Do
30	————————————————
8	————————————————
30	————————————————
9	————————————————
30	## To Do
10	————————————————
30	————————————————
11	————————————————
30	————————————————
12	## Routine Tasks
30	————————————————
1	————————————————
30	————————————————
2	————————————————
30	## Errands / Appointments
3	————————————————
30	————————————————
4	————————————————
30	————————————————
5	————————————————
30	
6	

Healthy Habits

Exercise: _____ Mins
Water O O O O O O O O

Daily Plan

Date   M T W Th F Sa Su

7a	
30	
8	
30	
9	
30	
10	
30	
11	
30	
12	
30	
1	
30	
2	
30	
3	
30	
4	
30	
5	
30	
6	

Must Do

To Do

Routine Tasks

Errands / Appointments

Healthy Habits

Exercise: _____ Mins

Water O O O O O O O O

Daily Plan

Date   M T W Th F Sa Su

7a	
30	
8	
30	
9	
30	
10	
30	
11	
30	
12	
30	
1	
30	
2	
30	
3	
30	
4	
30	
5	
30	
6	

Must Do

To Do

Routine Tasks

Errands / Appointments

Healthy Habits

Exercise: _____ Mins

Water O O O O O O O O

Daily Plan

Date M T W Th F Sa Su

Must Do

7a	
30	
8	
30	
9	

To Do

30
10
30
11
30
12
30

Routine Tasks

1
30
2
30
3
30
4
30

Errands / Appointments

5
30
6

Healthy Habits

Exercise: _____ Mins
Water O O O O O O O O

Daily Plan

Date   M T W Th F Sa Su

Must Do

7a ....

　30 _____

8 _____

　30 _____

9 _____

　30 _____

10 _____

　30 _____

11 _____

　30 _____

12 _____

　30 _____

1 _____

　30 _____

To Do

2 _____

　30 _____

3 _____

　30 _____

Routine Tasks

4 _____

　30 _____

5 _____

　30 _____

6 _____

Errands / Appointments

Healthy Habits

Exercise: _____ Mins

Water ⭘ ⭘ ⭘ ⭘ ⭘ ⭘ ⭘

Daily Plan

Date   M T W Th F Sa Su

Must Do

7a _____

30 _____

8 _____

30 _____

9 _____

30 _____

10 _____

To Do

30 _____

11 _____

30 _____

12 _____

30 _____

1 _____

Routine Tasks

30 _____

2 _____

30 _____

3 _____

30 _____

4 _____

30 _____

5 _____

Errands / Appointments

30 _____

6 _____

Healthy Habits

Exercise: _____ Mins

Water ⭕⭕⭕⭕⭕⭕⭕⭕

Daily Plan

Date

Must Do

7a ....

30 ....

8 ....

30 ....

9 ....

30 ....

10 ....

30 ....

To Do

11 ....

30 ....

12 ....

30 ....

1 ....

30 ....

Routine Tasks

2 ....

30 ....

3 ....

30 ....

4 ....

30 ....

5 ....

Errands / Appointments

30 ....

6 ....

Healthy Habits

Exercise: _____ Mins

Water ○ ○ ○ ○ ○ ○ ○ ○

_____ Week in Review

Top 3: Key Performance Indicators
These are the key measurables that are going to move the needle.

#1 Goal_____

Last Week   What must you do differently?

[   ] ⟹ [   ]

#2 Goal_____

Last Week   What must you do differently?

[   ] ⟹ [   ]

#3 Goal_____

Last Week   What must you do differently?

[   ] ⟹ [   ]

Digital Marketing Plan

CHAPTER 7: REFERRAL STRATEGY

This is basically capitalizing on the 80-20 rule. 80 percent of your income is going to come from 20 percent of your customers. The same thing goes for referrals. This is a 2 part strategy. First you want to provide a great experience and increase your income per customer. Second you want those customers to share your business and be happy to do so.

There are 100s of ways and ideas to get you customers to be your referral partners, but the big ones are discounts, incentives, added services, and other ways to make it a win-win.

Write this on your Wall...

Referrals are low-hanging fruit just waiting for you to harvest them.

Make Some Referral Goals

Area	Current	Future
Customer Service		
Reward Best Customers		
Shareable Experience		
Make It Easy to Share		
Referral Program		
Optimizing		

Big Referral GOAL _____

STEPS TO TAKE (ACTION)	BY WHEN	⊕

SMART GOALS – Specific, Measurable, Realistic, Achievable, Time-based.

What can you learn, outsource, simplify, automate or eliminate?

KEYS TO SUCCEESS (TASK)	WHO CAN HELP?	⊕

Daily Plan

Date   M T W Th F Sa Su

Must Do

7a ....

   30 ....

8 ....

   30 ....

9 ....

   30 ....

10 ....

   30 ....

11 ....

   30 ....

12 ....

   30 ....

1 ....

   30 ....

2 ....

   30 ....

3 ....

   30 ....

4 ....

   30 ....

5 ....

   30 ....

6 ....

Healthy Habits

Exercise: _____ Mins

Water ⭘ ⭘ ⭘ ⭘ ⭘ ⭘ ⭘ ⭘

To Do

Routine Tasks

Errands / Appointments

Daily Plan

Date

M T W Th F Sa Su

Must Do

7a

30

8

30

9

30

10

30

11

30

12

30

1

30

To Do

2

30

3

30

Routine Tasks

4

30

5

30

Errands / Appointments

6

Healthy Habits

Exercise: _____ Mins

Water O O O O O O O O

Daily Plan

Date   M T W Th F Sa Su

Must Do

7a ....

30 ....

8 ....

30 ....

9 ....

30 ....

To Do

10 ....

30 ....

11 ....

30 ....

12 ....

30 ....

1 ....

Routine Tasks

30 ....

2 ....

30 ....

3 ....

30 ....

4 ....

30 ....

5 ....

Errands / Appointments

30 ....

6 ....

Healthy Habits

Exercise: _____ Mins

Water O O O O O O O O

Daily Plan

Date   M T W Th F Sa Su

7a	## Must Do
30	
8	
30	
9	
30	
10	## To Do
30	
11	
30	
12	
30	
1	
30	## Routine Tasks
2	
30	
3	
30	
4	
30	
5	## Errands / Appointments
30	
6	

Healthy Habits

Exercise: _____ Mins
Water ○ ○ ○ ○ ○ ○ ○ ○

Daily Plan

Date   M T W Th F Sa Su

Must Do

7a ....

30 ....

8 ....

30 ....

9 ....

30 ....

To Do

10 ....

30 ....

11 ....

30 ....

12 ....

30 ....

1 ....

Routine Tasks

30 ....

2 ....

30 ....

3 ....

30 ....

4 ....

30 ....

5 ....

Errands / Appointments

30 ....

6 ....

Healthy Habits

Exercise: _____ Mins

Water ⭕ ⭕ ⭕ ⭕ ⭕ ⭕ ⭕ ⭕

Daily Plan

Date

Must Do

| 7a |
| 30 |
| 8 |
| 30 |
| 9 |
| 30 |

To Do

| 10 |
| 30 |
| 11 |
| 30 |
| 12 |
| 30 |

Routine Tasks

| 1 |
| 30 |
| 2 |
| 30 |
| 3 |
| 30 |

| 4 |
| 30 |
| 5 |
| 30 |

Errands / Appointments

| 6 |

Healthy Habits

Exercise: _____ Mins

Water O O O O O O O O

Daily Plan

Date   M T W Th F Sa Su

Must Do

7a ....
  30 ....
8 ....
  30 ....
9 ....
  30 ....

To Do

10 ....
  30 ....
11 ....
  30 ....
12 ....
  30 ....
1 ....

Routine Tasks

  30 ....
2 ....
  30 ....
3 ....
  30 ....
4 ....
  30 ....

Errands / Appointments

5 ....
  30 ....
6 ....

Healthy Habits

Exercise: _____ Mins
Water O O O O O O O O

_____ Week in Review

Top 3: Key Performance Indicators
These are the key measurables that are going to move the needle.

#1 Goal_____

Last Week

What must you do differently?

#2 Goal_____

Last Week

What must you do differently?

#3 Goal_____

Last Week

What must you do differently?

CHAPTER 8: REPUTATION STRATEGY

Online Reputation Management is an intensive process that businesses follow to ensure that their online reputation is solid and protected by:

- ✓ **"Building"** a strong brand image
- ✓ **"Recovering"** from a tarnished online image
- ✓ **"Maintaining"** a long-term, consistent initiative

The Secret Ingredient For SUCCESS

Make Some Reputation Goals

Area	Current	Future
Facebook Reviews		
Google Reviews		
Testimonials		
Brand Awareness		
Encourage Positive Reviews		
Monitor what is said		

Big Reputation GOAL _____

STEPS TO TAKE (ACTION)	BY WHEN	⊕

SMART GOALS – Specific, Measurable, Realistic, Achievable, Time-based.

What can you learn, outsource, simplify, automate or eliminate?

KEYS TO SUCCEESS (TASK)	WHO CAN HELP?	⊕

Daily Plan

Date   M T W Th F Sa Su

Must Do

_____

7a _____

30 _____

8   _____

30 _____

9   _____

30 _____

To Do

10 _____

30 _____

11 _____

30 _____

12 _____

30 _____

1   _____

Routine Tasks

30 _____

2   _____

30 _____

3   _____

30 _____

4   _____

30 _____

5   _____

Errands / Appointments

30 _____

6   _____

Healthy Habits

Exercise: _____ Mins

Water O O O O O O O O

Daily Plan

Date   M T W Th F Sa Su

Must Do

_____
_____
_____
_____
_____

To Do

7a _____
  30 _____
8 _____
  30 _____
9 _____
  30 _____

_____
_____
_____
_____

10 _____
  30 _____
11 _____
  30 _____
12 _____
  30 _____

Routine Tasks

1 _____
  30 _____
2 _____
  30 _____
3 _____
  30 _____

_____
_____
_____
_____

4 _____
  30 _____
5 _____
  30 _____
6 _____

Errands / Appointments

Healthy Habits

Exercise: _____ Mins
Water O O O O O O O O

_____
_____
_____
_____

Daily Plan

Date   M   T W Th F Sa Su

7a ....

  30 ....

8 ....

  30 ....

9 ....

  30 ....

10 ....

  30 ....

11 ....

  30 ....

12 ....

  30 ....

1 ....

  30 ....

2 ....

  30 ....

3 ....

  30 ....

4 ....

  30 ....

5 ....

  30 ....

6 ....

Healthy Habits

Exercise: _____ Mins

Water O O O O O O O O

Must Do

To Do

Routine Tasks

Errands / Appointments

Daily Plan

Date

Must Do

7a

30

8

30

9

30

To Do

10

30

11

30

12

30

1

30

Routine Tasks

2

30

3

30

4

30

5

Errands / Appointments

30

6

Healthy Habits

Exercise: _____ Mins

Water ○ ○ ○ ○ ○ ○ ○ ○

Daily Plan

Date   M T W Th F Sa Su

Must Do

7a ....

30 ....

8 ....

30 ....

9 ....

30 ....

10 ....

To Do

30 ....

11 ....

30 ....

12 ....

30 ....

1 ....

Routine Tasks

30 ....

2 ....

30 ....

3 ....

30 ....

4 ....

30 ....

5 ....

Errands / Appointments

30 ....

6 ....

Healthy Habits

Exercise: _____ Mins

Water ⭘ ⭘ ⭘ ⭘ ⭘ ⭘ ⭘ ⭘

Daily Plan

Date

Must Do

| 7a |
| 30 |
| 8 |
| 30 |
| 9 |
| 30 |

To Do

| 10 |
| 30 |
| 11 |
| 30 |
| 12 |
| 30 |

Routine Tasks

| 1 |
| 30 |
| 2 |
| 30 |
| 3 |
| 30 |
| 4 |
| 30 |
| 5 |

Errands / Appointments

| 30 |
| 6 |

Healthy Habits

Exercise: _____ Mins

Water ○ ○ ○ ○ ○ ○ ○ ○

Daily Plan

Date

Must Do

7a	
30	
8	
30	
9	
30	
10	
30	
11	
30	
12	
30	
1	
30	
2	
30	
3	
30	
4	
30	
5	
30	
6	

To Do

Routine Tasks

Errands / Appointments

Healthy Habits

Exercise: _____ Mins

Water O O O O O O O O

_____ Week in Review

Top 3: Key Performance Indicators
These are the key measurables that are going to move the needle.

#1 Goal_____

Last Week   What must you do differently?

```
┌──────────┐        ┌──────────────────┐
│          │   ⇒    │                  │
│          │        │                  │
└──────────┘        └──────────────────┘
```

#2 Goal_____

Last Week   What must you do differently?

```
┌──────────┐        ┌──────────────────┐
│          │   ⇒    │                  │
│          │        │                  │
└──────────┘        └──────────────────┘
```

#3 Goal_____

Last Week   What must you do differently?

```
┌──────────┐        ┌──────────────────┐
│          │   ⇒    │                  │
│          │        │                  │
└──────────┘        └──────────────────┘
```

PREP WORK FOR FUTURE

Now that you are well into your Video & Email Strategies, it is time to look back and forward at your goals. You have covered your digital footprint, but now it is time to really focus on the 4 growth factors.

By focusing on your referral & reputation strategies next, you will be ahead of a lot of business that never develop either of these strategies. These are keys to long-term success.

Make Some Goals

Area	Current	Future
Website		
Local		
Social		
Video		
Email		
Referral		
Reputation		

Notes:

PRIMARY GROWTH FACTORS

1. Customer Acquisition

Attracting new customers is the lifeline for any business and should be an on-going initiative.

2. Customer Retention

Getting your satisfied customers to keep coming back is critical and less expensive than acquisition.

3. Increased Spending

Getting your existing customers to spend more money with your company creates more automated revenue.

4. Increased Referrals

Getting your existing customers to refer more people to your business creates effortless longevity and growth.

Digital Marketing Plan

CHAPTER 9: LAST 4 WEEKS IN REVIEW

Now that you are started on all your Web Growth Strategies it is time to look back and forward at your goals. You might be excited, but you might need another month or year to feel like you've got a handle on all of this.

At this point you should be comfortable enough with all you have learned to be able to make decisions more freely on what to outsource and eliminate to make your strategy work for you. Let's review your KPIs first.

Make Notes in your plan to Achieve your Goals

KPIs	Goal	WK1	WK2	WK3	WK4
Traffic					
Leads					
Sales					
Gross Revenue					
Social KPI					
Local KPI					
Page #1					
# of Online Assets					

REVIEW SUCCESS from Last 8 Weeks

In order to plan for the next Year/8 weeks ahead you need to get clear on what's been going on this year - the good and the not so good. We can learn so many amazing lessons from doing this, so let's begin...

Firstly, let's kick off with a celebration - what have you achieved this year? What's going well? What are you most proud of? What do you want to celebrate? Write it all down...

_____

_____

_____

_____

_____

_____

_____

Now do a happy dance! Celebrate, pat yourself on the back, really take it all in. As entrepreneurs we rarely have anyone else to call us out on our successes and to encourage us to celebrate, so I'm calling you out now. Let's feel good about what has gone right this year.

REVIEW HABITS from Last 8 Weeks

Take a moment and think about who you had to be, to achieve these things. What kind of things did you do? Really think about your behavior, habits and attitude and write about the part of you that created this success...

_____

_____

_____

_____

_____

_____

_____

Our success is created from the inside out - it's who we're being that's determining what we're creating and achieving. So, the more we understand ourselves and what's going on, inside your head, the more we can tweak our behavior for success.

REVIEW FRUSTRATIONS from Last 8 Weeks

Ok, so now we're clear on that, let's look at the not so good stuff. What didn't go so well for you? What did you want to achieve but didn't? What frustrated you the most? Write it down...

_____

_____

_____

_____

We can learn so much from the things that didn't turn out the way we'd hoped.

REVIEW FEARS

Now, let's go inwards. What fears, worries, or doubts did you have that held you back? What thought was it that kept you playing small (if that's something you felt happened this year)? What habits and behaviors fueled the not so good happening?

_____

_____

_____

_____

Make the decision that you're going to let go of being this person. Just because you behaved this way in the past does not mean that you have to behave the same way in the future. New month, new start, new you. The more aware you are of the behavior that holds you back, the more you can let go and move forward in a more powerful way.

GOALS

Now it's time to get clear about what you truly want to make happen in the future.

DREAM Big

I want you to ease into your goals for next Year/8 weeks by having a dreaming session. What do you want it to look like? What would you love to have happen to say, "that was a GREAT Year/8 weeks"?

Dream big & write down what you want.

_____

_____

_____

_____

_____

_____

_____

_____

_____

_____

Dream it. Do It.

SO NOW YOU HAVE THE BIG PICTURE,

LET'S BREAK IT DOWN FOR YOUR BUSINESS...

What are your top 3 goals in your business right now?

Write them down in the order of their importance:

#1_____

#2_____

#3_____

Your PLAN

Let's make your plan, but before we do, you need to ask yourself what are the individual steps that you need to do to get there? What skills do you need to develop to take your business to the next level? Really think about this one. If you want to 2x your business next month through email marketing, but you don't even have a CRM system set-up, or you don't know what a CRM system is, you need help.

Sometimes it is a great advantage in business to outsource a lot of your needs so that you can get where you want faster. You might think it's crazy to spend money on others doing the work, when you know you can learn it. When those thoughts creep in, remind yourself you are not "spending money", you are **investing** in your business. You must invest money rather than time to get to the next level faster and more efficiently than you could do it on your own.

You don't need to know how you're going to do everything, but you need to plan as much as you can, so your goal isn't so overwhelming.

GOAL #1_____

STEPS TO TAKE (ACTION)	BY WHEN	⊕

SMART GOALS – Specific, Measurable, Realistic, Achievable, Time-based.

What can you learn, outsource, simplify, automate or eliminate?

KEYS TO SUCCEESS (TASK)	WHO CAN HELP?	⊕

GOAL #2_____

STEPS TO TAKE (ACTION)	BY WHEN	⊕

SMART GOALS – Specific, Measurable, Realistic, Achievable, Time-based.

What can you learn, outsource, simplify, automate or eliminate?

KEYS TO SUCCEESS (TASK)	WHO CAN HELP?	⊕

GOAL #3_____

STEPS TO TAKE (ACTION)	BY WHEN	⊕

SMART GOALS – Specific, Measurable, Realistic, Achievable, Time-based.

What can you learn, outsource, simplify, automate or eliminate?

KEYS TO SUCCEESS (TASK)	WHO CAN HELP?	⊕

Ready for the Next 8 Weeks!

The only thing that's going to get you to where you want next year is YOU. So, let's plan for how you're going to be the best version of yourself for your Future.   This is the mental part.

What are the biggest things that will stop you from getting to where you want?

_____

_____

_____

What will it take to stay on track?

_____

_____

_____

What's going to be your motto for the year?

_____

_____

_____

You can achieve the most wonderful things. Just stay focused on what you want and step into the power that's already within you to play big and make it happen. Success is not an accident and I know that you're going to make it happen on purpose.

NOTES/IDEAS

Digital Marketing Plan

Digital Marketing Plan

Digital Marketing Plan

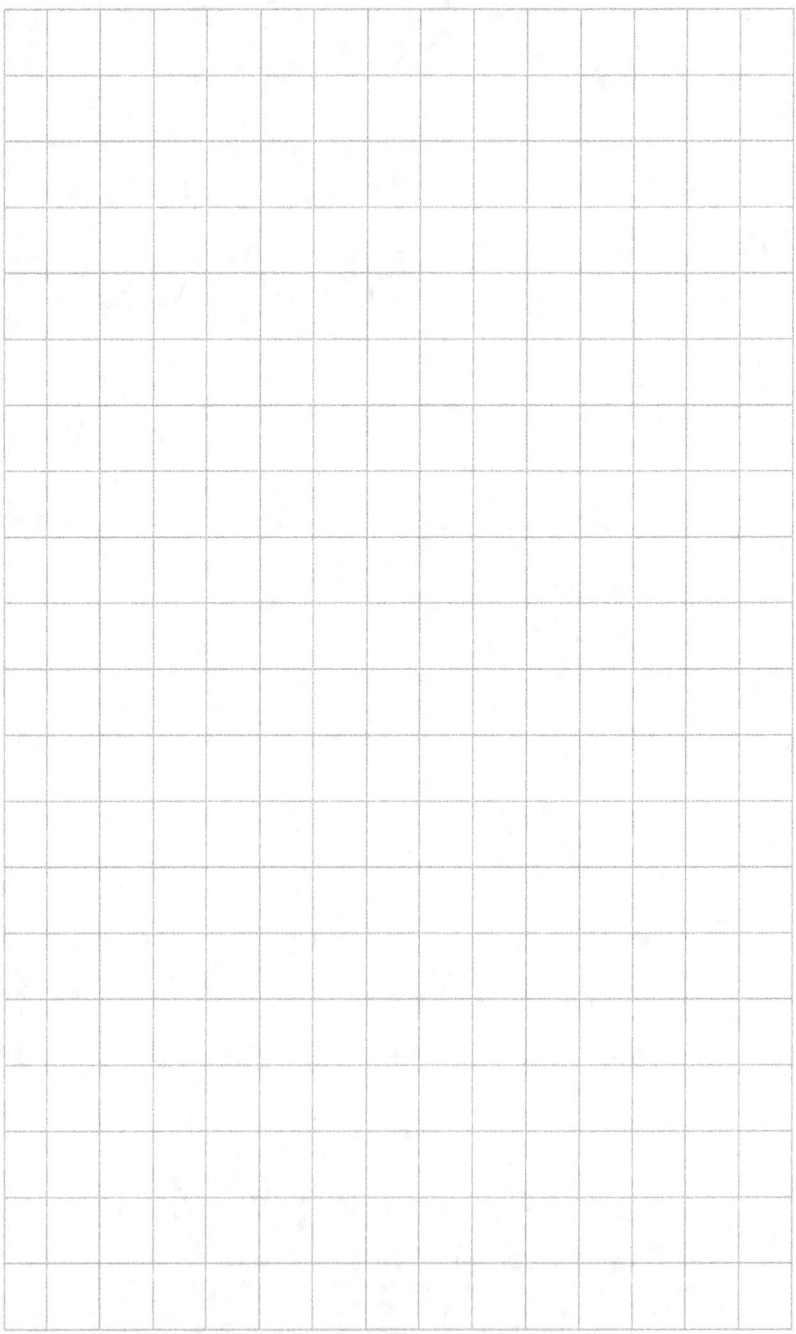

Digital Marketing Plan

Digital Marketing Plan

Digital Marketing Plan

Digital Marketing Plan

Digital Marketing Plan

Digital Marketing Plan

Digital Marketing Plan

Digital Marketing Plan

Digital Marketing Plan

Digital Marketing Plan

Digital Marketing Plan

Digital Marketing Plan

Digital Marketing Plan

Digital Marketing Plan

Digital Marketing Plan

Digital Marketing Plan

Digital Marketing Plan

Digital Marketing Plan

AUTHOR NOTE

I would love to continue the journey with you

and help you to make your most successful year yet! You are invited to learn how your business can pay for its own growth.

With over 400 successful projects with returns of 2x-10x the initial investment, you can plan on profit.

You determine what you want to profit. Together we setup a strategy to guarantee it.

Set-up a FREE strategy call (including a full SEO review) with me at

Https://pambillups.com

And let's talk more.

www.ingramcontent.com/pod-product-compliance
Lightning Source LLC
Chambersburg PA
CBHW070342220526
45467CB00001B/220